Flower Dance

Beautiful Appliqué Using No-Fail Techniques

Flower Dance

Beautiful Appliqué Using No-Fail Techniques

By Hallye Bone
Edited by Judy Pearlstein
Technical Editing by Kathe Doughtery
Design by Kelly Ludwig
Photographs by Aaron Leimkuehler
Illustrations by Lon Eric Craven
Production Assistance by Jo Ann Groves

Location photos at Powell Gardens,
Kingsville, Missouri
powellgardens.org

Published by Kansas City Star Books
1729 Grand Boulevard
Kansas City, Missouri 64108

First edition, first printing
ISBN: 9781935362753
Library of Congress number: 2010939978

Printed in the United States of America
By Walsworth Publishing Co.
Marceline, Missouri

To order copies, call StarInfo, 816-234-4636
(say "Operator)

KANSAS CITY STAR BOOKS

www.Pickledish.com

The Quilter's Home Page

Table of Contents

Flower Dance Block Pattern Index

About the Author

Hallye Bone began quilting in 1967 and has been teaching students how to appliqué for more than thirty years. She now teaches quilt making techniques throughout the U. S. She is the author of *Caring for Your Quilts*, a classic reference book, published by Kansas City Star Books. She has written for quilting magazines for 15 years. She is an appraiser of quilted textiles, certified by the American Quilter's Society in Paducah. Hallye lectures and teaches workshops across the country about vintage quilts, quilts' history, and methods of quilt making. Her designs have appeared in national magazines. She quilts every day and repairs beloved quilted heirlooms for clients.

Introduction and Acknowledgements

Flower Dance began as a block of the month for Patches Quilt Shop in St. Charles, Missouri. The project grew in size and stretched over three years. I decided the patterns could be gathered into book form. It not only takes a village to raise a child, it took lots of help to turn my flower drawings into a book.

Special thanks to Wendy Sprague at the Brick Path B & B in Berkeley, California, where I first began sketching the flowers in her charming garden. Ellen O'Bryan in Hannibal, Missouri, suggested using a high-contrast black background to make the bright Moda fabric flowers pop. Sharon Brader, Dolores Keaton, and Dena Mullet made samples. My husband Merle encouraged me to keep writing. Ann Hazelwood, former owner of Patches Quilt Shop, was an inspiration and advisor during the blocks' design process. Pat Waelder, owner of the amazing Hickory Stick Quilt Shop in Hannibal, Missouri, gave me ideas for projects to use those designs.

I sincerely thank my editor Judy Pearlstein for her talent and patience. I am blessed to have the talented Kelly Ludwig as art designer. She made the design process a world of "yes." Photographer Aaron Leimkuehler had the job of making everything beautiful and clear to the reader — he did a great job! And a big thank you to Kathe Dougherty, technical editor, for catching errors. Kudos to Lon Eric Craven for illustrating the patterns and diagrams. Thank you to Jo Ann Groves for production assistance, and to Bill Elliott for taking my photo.

Powell Gardens, east of Kansas City, Missouri, is the scene of some of our photos, and is not to be missed — it's a fascinating place! (And, be sure to visit Prairie Point Quilt Shop in Shawnee, Kansas. We shot some photos there too, where Kathy Delaney was the perfect hand model.)

My former editor and friend Edie McGinnis extended her humor and help when I needed it most. Doug Weaver, former publisher of the Kansas City Star Books, has been a welcome advisor, friend and mentor. Thanks, too, to my sister Dr. Emilie Bergmann of Berkeley, California, my critic, editor and a talented, new quilter! Jean Ameduri shared her super pillowcase instructions — thanks! My late mother, Hilda Bergmann, a renowned artist, taught me to draw and to see nature in new ways. Her talent for nurturing and growing things is her legacy to me and I am grateful to her daily.

For 45 fabulous years, quilting has opened the doors to a supportive group of generous, creative people. My quilting friends and students are the special flowers in my life's garden. Thanks to you all.

Emerson said that "earth laughs in flowers," and flowered quilts celebrate nature's spectacular, varied beauty. A lifelong love of flowers inspired the designs for Flower Dance.

When you stitch the Flower Dance blooms, you'll create a lasting treasure and you'll enjoy nature's bounty all year long. You can choose from unusual blossoms like fuchsia or old favorites like daisies and roses. For the holidays, try the poinsettia block. These designs are versatile — make a throw for a favorite gardener, an apron for a friend, a tote bag, or appliqué all of the blocks for a masterpiece quilt. Let your projects document your own garden's progress or "plant" a fantasy garden in fabric. The patterns can be hand appliquéd or fused and embellished by machine or by hand. As a bonus, these line drawing designs are simple enough to be used for redwork or outline embroidery. They make stunning pillowcases, aprons, table runners, and purses. They can be enlarged or reduced in size, as your project requires.

Techniques

Appliqué

Appliqué looks like a challenge. Thirty years ago, I was intimidated by it. I taught a basic quilt making class for eleven years and always choked before the session when I had to teach appliqué. One day, I got to class early and discovered a way to simplify appliqué, a method that works for me. I get feedback from my students who say that my "No-Fail" hand appliqué has freed them from dreading appliqué. This book should help you overcome any reluctance you have in trying appliqué. Remember, there are no quilt police to catch any small glitches in your stitching. Step back from your work occasionally. You won't see your mistakes and you'll see the big picture and enjoy making fabric bloom.

No-Fail Hand Appliqué

Appliqué is freeing, relaxing, and portable. The word appliqué means "to apply." When you appliqué, you are really painting a picture by applying fabric. Anything you can draw can be translated into appliqué. The basic goal is to make your stitches as unobtrusive as possible (ideally, invisible) and yet as secure as possible. There are many appliqué methods. My own technique uses thin cardboard and an iron. If you have a method that works for you, use it instead. But before you reject it, try the cardboard/heat method in one or two blocks and then decide.

The concept: Turning appliqué fabric shapes under with the aid of an iron and a thin cardboard template. With this method, your shapes are exactly those in the pattern. It's ideal for making multiples of a single shape as in Sunbonnet Sue. To look balanced, each Sue's bonnet, dress, hat and arm must be the same. The cardboard template/heat method makes each piece symmetrical and identical.

For No-Fail Appliqué, You Will Need:

1. #10 crewel or embroidery needles (I prefer John James, Hemmings or Colonial) unless you're stitching through fabric AND a fusible. When you're sewing through many thicknesses, use a #8 or #9 needle to prevent the needle bending and breaking.

2. 50 or 60 wt. cotton thread to match each color of appliqué OR matching silk thread (Silk is costly but it becomes almost invisible when sewn into the edge of an applique.) I use Mettler "Silk-Finish" cotton in thread to match each appliqué. (Green thread for green leaves, red thread for red tulip petals, etc.)

3. Thin, silk pins (I like IBC pins because they're thin and they won't add extra bulk.)

4. Scissors — two kinds:
   a. small, sharp embroidery scissors or snips and
   b. medium sized sewing shears

5. Thin cardboard — file folders work well.

6. Iron — without steam. Small craft irons work well.

7. Fabric: 100% cotton fabric in various colors for floral appliqués. Effective appliqués begin with interesting, marbled or subtly printed fabrics. From a distance, the fabrics may look like solid colors but close examination reveals gradations of color. For **Flower Dance**, I used many shades of Moda's Marbles. Part of the fun of creating the designs was choosing the fabrics. Other fabrics like Robert Kaufman's "Fusions" or Andover's "Dimples" work well, too.

8. If desired, use spray starch before you cut out the appliqués from the fabric.

9. Square appliqué base fabric, 2" larger than the finished block size.

10. Markers: Chalk marker for a black base fabric or blue wash-out marker for white or light fabrics. Chalk should be white; don't use colored chalk or markers as they may not wash out.

11. All fabrics used for appliqué should be prewashed.

Steps to No-Fail Appliqué
Using the template/heat method

Before you begin, if you wish, you may enlarge the flower designs. My goal was to keep the flowers small. You can enlarge the patterns up to 25% and still keep the designs within the 10" block. You have permission to copy and enlarge the designs to make them easier to handle and to appliqué. However, you are not permitted to sell the designs or patterns or share them with friends without permission.

1. Xerox or trace flower design onto paper.

2. Analyze each design. Find the lowest point and determine the order in which the pieces should be laid down. *Example:* in a daisy, the stems and leaves should be appliquéd first, peeking out from beneath the petals. Then, you will attach the flower's petals, and last, you will add the daisy's center.

3. Trace the flower design onto the base fabric by laying the fabric on the design. Use a light box or window on a sunny day to see designs through dark fabric. If you use black background fabric, use a white chalk pencil. Masking tape will hold the design and fabric in place on your light source. A glass-topped table with a light underneath works well. But don't place the light close to the glass.

4. Cut design elements (petals, leaves) from the paper pattern. Trace onto thin cardboard and cut out.

5. Place cardboard template (right side down) onto the wrong side of the appliqué fabric. Trace and cut out the petal, leaf or stem, leaving a generous ¼" seam allowance around each. Don't skimp on the seam allowance; each piece not only has to have enough fibers to hold your stitches, it also has to be able to work around the cardboard templates. Do not clip convex (outward) curves; they will turn under without help. Clip only the concave (inward) curves and sharp dips.

Do not clip through the traced line because you want enough fibers to hold your stitches, even at the design dips. Lay the cardboard template on the wrong side of the fabric, positioning it in place on the fabric with your finger. Using the iron, carefully work the seam allowance over the cardboard.

Avoid steam in your iron; steam can burn your fingers. Remove cardboard.

6. Position the turned-edge appliqué pieces onto the background fabric, using the traced design as a guide. Pin pieces in place, using silk pins, OR use Roxanne's Glue Baste-It.

Use only tiny droplets of this glue to anchor the appliqués. *Note:* This must be washed out with cool water after you attach the appliqué. Gently work out the glue in water with your fingers after you've finished stitching. Pat with a towel and allow to dry.

7. As you stitch, to manipulate appliqués, try using a flat wooden toothpick (its tiny splinters will grab fabric fibers). I also use "That Purple Thang," or Alex Anderson's tool with a stiletto and seam ripper to coax fabric into the shapes I want.

8. Using a blind-hem stitch and matching thread, sew the appliqués onto the background fabric.

9. Master leaves' points: The *Flower Dance* designs use many leaves, requiring you to master appliquéd points. Two methods of appliquéing a pointed leaf, heart, or other design are detailed on page 10.

10. Finally, to add accents, embellish or embroider as each design requires — with a variety of stitches for veins, petals, flowers' centers.

Mastering Leaf Points

Cut out the appliqué, leaving a generous ¼" seam allowance. Lay the appliqué's right side of the fabric on an ironing board. Place the cardboard template on the wrong side of fabric. Hold in place with your index finger or stilleto. Work the fabric around the cardboard, pressing the seam allowance toward the center of the appliqué. When you get to the point, first turn one side of the point. Press. Then turn the other side of the appliqué. Press. Usually, there will be a small amount of unturned fabric remaining. Remove the cardboard and press that remaining loose bit of fabric under, creating a third fold.

Allow the iron to rest on these three folds for 2-3 seconds to heat-set the point. To secure a pointed appliqué onto fabric, bring your thread up at the appliqué's point and sew one stitch to anchor it. Then appliqué the rest of the leaf as usual.

A second method is to first lay the appliqué wrong side down. Turn under the seam allowance at the tip of the leaf and at its base. Press. Next, turn and press each side of the leaf, using the cardboard template as your guide. Turn the appliqué over and press on the right side to set the turned seam allowances.

For dips or other sharp v-like designs as in hearts, after turning the applique's edges, make one short clip right at the place where the dip occurs but stay one or two threads away from the appliqué's turning edge so these threads act as an anchor for your stitches. There is no need to clip around the curved portion of the appliqué; it should turn naturally with the iron's heat. Clipping fewer times means less fraying, a drawback in appliqué.

Putting Personality into Each Flower

When cutting the petals, centers and leaf shapes, add a dash of personality. Go to the garden or a greenhouse and really study flowers. They aren't perfect. Some petals are wider than others, some longer. They may lean to one side. Don't worry about a "mistake" in appliquéing flowers. There are no mistakes in nature and, if your flowers are a little off-kilter, they will look more natural. Of course, when you're doing stylized or folk art appliqué, flowers need to be rounded and look more like lollipops. In these *Flower Dance* appliqués, your aim is grace and realism. Here's how to make your appliqués more real:

1. Cut "round" flower centers slightly oval and occasionally angle the flower's center slightly.

2. Give your petals personality by making leaves bend slightly and gently, curving them as nature does.

3. More personality can be added with curved, slightly meandering embroidered veins along the leaves' centers.

4. When embroidering stamens, pistils, or seeds in flowers' centers, use more than one color of floss. I rarely use black floss for flowers' centers; it's usually too harsh. I often use one dark brown strand and one strand of lighter brown. This old trick will give highlights to the finished embroidery. Inexpensive cotton floss resembles silk.

5. If you can't find an exact match of a flower in embroidery floss, mix two closely related shades, one strand of each.

6. Step back from your work to get the big picture. You'll see every mis-stitch if you're ten inches away. Needlework looks different from a distance. Pin the block on your design wall and see how it looks from a distance.

Enhanced, Embroidered Embellishment

The concept: This technique requires that every appliquéd piece is outlined in embroidery. Petals' shapes sometimes blur when they are next to one another and embroidered embellishment helps to keep each petal, stem or leaf distinct. After you complete all pieces in an appliqué flower, add outline embroidery in matching thread around each piece to add accents to the flowers' petals and leaves. The bonus is that, if your appliques' edges aren't perfectly curved, outline embroidery will cover the flaws. For the enhanced embellishment technique, use the "outline" or "stem" stitch. Choose either two or three strands of floss. Three strands will create a bold outline; using two strands is more subtle. This style of embroidery with appliqué is becoming popular among prize-winning quilt makers like Suzanne Marshall.

Blind-Hem Applique Stitch

The concept: Invisible stitching to attach appliqués to base fabric. Blind-hemming is virtually invisible and is quicker than the whip stitch because you are taking several stitches at once. Use thread that matches each appliqué to insure invisible stitches. Example: green thread for leaves, red for tulip petals. Knot thread with a single loop, run knot into the appliqué's crease to secure and hide it. Begin attaching the appliqué by running the thread ¼" into the crease of the appliqué and then ¼" into the background fabric. Continue around the entire appliqué. To anchor thread at the end of the applique, stitch over the first stitches, about 1". Take only one or two stitches on the needle when stitching around curves. As you appliqué along straight lines, take four or five stitches on the needle. This method is also called the "ladder" stitch. An alternative appliqué stitch is the "whip" stitch. However, stitches are more apt to show if the whip stitch is used. If you choose to use it, practice until your stitches are even.

Perfect Circular Applique Shapes

The concept: The goal is to make a smoothly curved appliqué. The method is similar to making covered buttons, using a basting stitch. To get a perfect circle or oval, cut appliqué fabric a generous ¼" larger than the cardboard template. Using a light colored thread and a running stitch, baste between the circle's raw edge and the marked turning line.

Place the cardboard circle shape onto the wrong side of the fabric. Hold in place with your finger. Gently pull the basting thread to gather the fabric around the circular cardboard shape.

Press with a hot, dry iron, still holding the basting thread. Wait a moment to cool the cardboard inside the appliqué. Then, loosen the basting thread and carefully slip the cardboard out. Press on the right side to set the appliqué's crease.

Hint: Press all appliqués for a single flower at one time and store in a tin or a zip-loc bag until you're ready to appliqué.

Speedy Stems

The concept: Eliminate a step when you appliqué straight lines and stems. Simplify appliquéd stems and other narrow lines, curved or straight. Here's how:

1. Trace the stem placement onto base fabric.

2. Cut the stem, ½" wide, on the appliqué fabric's <u>bias</u>. You will trim this later. It's easier to work with a half inch and trim later, after one side of the stem is sewn down.

3. Pin the stem along one side, curving it as the design indicates.

Using a running stitch, sew 1/8" away from the raw edge.

For a very narrow stem, trim close to the stitching, leaving only two or three threads.

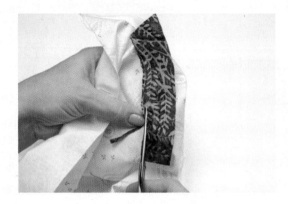

Next, turn the stem over and finger press.

4. Trim the other side of the stem, leaving 1/8" for appliqué and 1/16" for turning under. Carefully turn the stem's edges, pin,

and appliqué the second side down.

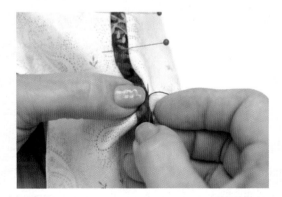

5. If desired, press the stem. However, I usually don't press this because I like a slightly rounded, dimensional look for stems.

Applique Hints

1. Batiks: Because they are so closely woven, batiks aren't usually the best choice for appliqués. It's more difficult to drive the needle through a batik and get a smooth, even stitch. If a batik is the perfect color choice, use it, keeping in mind that you may have sore fingers from driving the needle through the close weave.

2. Don't be afraid to try glues to keep appliqués in place. Just be sure to get all traces of glue out before completing your project.

3. Use marbled fabrics for a more interesting appliqué.

Other Applique Methods

Needleturn Appliqué

The concept: To do needleturn, you need only a sewing (size #10 Crewel or embroidery) needle, thread, and your thumb nail. Cut out the appliqué, adding a scant ¼" seam allowance. Mark the placement on the base fabric, using chalk on dark fabric or a wash-out blue marker on light fabric. Hold the appliqué down with your thumbnail. Using the needle to manipulate and to turn under a scant ¼" seam allowance, turn edges of the appliqué and stitch down to the base fabric. Use a blind hem stitch or a whip-stitch, making sure that the stitches are evenly spaced if they show on the top of your work. Problems can occur with needleturn appliqué when stitching around a curve. Because fabrics' fibers are straight, fabric may not curve smoothly; care must be taken to create a curved edge. Finger pressing as you work can help. And, practice is the key to this method.

Freezer Paper Appliqué

The concept: Using an iron, the shiny side of freezer paper is fused to the wrong side of appliqué shapes.(Reverse the pattern before cutting.) A scant ¼" seam is turned under with an iron, using the freezer paper as a guide. As the appliqué is sewn down to the base, the freezer paper is removed. You might wish to glue or starch the seam allowance to keep it turned. *Suggestions:* Apply liquid starch with a small brush. Or use Roxanne's Glue-Baste-It. When using this product, the bottle has a small needlelike tip for applying tiny pindot drops of glue. Let dry and, after appliqués are stitched, gently rub out the starch or glue under cool water.

Fused Appliqué

Fusibles have become popular as a way to quickly make an appliquéd design. Carefully read the directions of the fusible; each one is different. For example, Pellon's Wonder-Under requires first a 3-second, high heat setting to fuse its sticky, rough side to the fabric. After fusing, peel off the paper backing, cut out the appliqué, and place it on the base fabric. Last, using a damp press cloth and an iron's high heat setting, hold the iron down on the appliqué for 10-15 seconds to set it onto the base fabric. Embellish as desired.

Raw Edge Fused Appliqué

Today's raw edge appliqué uses fusibles. Often used in vintage quilts, raw edge appliqué was quick but edges of the appliqué often frayed after repeated washings. Fused, raw edge appliqués may not last forever and we don't know whether the glues will become brittle through the years. It's still a great way to speed the appliqué process, though. Fuse the appliqué onto the background fabric. Then embellish by hand, stitching the blanket, buttonhole, or running stitch close to the edge of the appliqué. Use a larger needle (# 8 or # 9) to drive through all thicknesses and the fusible, OR machine embellish edges, using your machine's buttonhole or blanket stitch. Consult your machine's guide book for the manufacturer's recommendations. My Bernina recommends an open-toe foot when using the buttonhole stitch. I use a 70/10 "Sharp" OR a Microtex needle. The reason is that a sharp needle will make a smaller hole in appliqués, it can drive through more thicknesses, and is more efficient. Before you begin, practice on some waste fabric so you can get an even stitch length and the desired stitch width. I like to use black thread for decorative buttonhole stitching but often use thread that matches the appliqué. To avoid puckering the appliqué and to keep the fabric taut, lay a piece of Tear Away Stabilizer or Floriani stabilizer on the back of your work. Remove it when you're finished stitching. Use the same color thread in your bobbin as your top thread to avoid unsightly bobbin thread showing up on the top of your work.

Invisible Machine-Stitched Appliqué

Using your machine's guide book, check out their stitch recommendations for invisible machine appliqué. Important: Use polyester invisible thread, not nylon. Nylon will melt if an iron or hot steam gets near it. If you use cotton thread, use thread that matches each appliqué. The machine is programmed to take several stitches between the appliqué stitches. Practice on waste fabric so you can take only one single thread along the side of the appliqué and several tiny stitches between it and the next stitch. Again, practice is the key to getting the look you want.

Redwork (Outline Embroidery) Tips

Flower Dance designs were designed to be embroidered as well as appliqued. I love the relaxing, rhythmic stitching of redwork or outline embroidery. Medical experts say that repetitive sewing, knitting or embroidery lowers blood pressure and heart rate. So, embroidery is a healthy hobby! Nine basic embroidery stitches are shown on pages 40-41. Here are some tips to improve your finished work:

1.   To trace outline embroidery designs, use a Gelly Roll, Pigma or other

indelible, fine-pointed pen. Gelly Rolls and Pigmas are made to roll smoothly over the threads of cotton fabrics. Match, as closely as possible, the pen to the embroidery thread's color. Then, it won't matter if the embroidery stitching doesn't completely cover these markings; the inked lines will blend with your thread.

2. Floss tip: Find the grain of the floss (using a magnifying glass, if necessary). Note the direction of the fibers. Thread the needle so that the thread goes with the grain. No more rough-looking stitches.

3. To avoid knots and tangles in handwork, draw floss through "Thread Heaven," available at quilting and embroidery shops.

4. To replicate the blue-red stitches popular in the late 1800's, use DMC #498.

5. Use 1, 2, or 3 strands, depending on the project. One strand works for tiny details like eyes, facial features, veins of leaves and windows of buildings. Two strands work well for most projects. Three strands create a bold line. I used two strands throughout this book's projects but for a bolder line, use three strands.

6. Don't allow floss to "travel" across the backing fabric or run it from one part of the design to another. It will show through and detract from the design. A solution is to lay a piece of batiste on the back of the base fabric. Clip thread ends close to the knots or thread starts to avoid these showing through to the front of your work. In past centuries, needle workers prided themselves on the back of the embroidery looking as good as the front. They had more time than we do to create perfection. But today's stitcher wants to guard against wayward threads on the back of embroidery work as they can inadvertently be drawn to the top, creating unsightly problems.

7. Test color fastness of floss if you're in doubt by wetting a small portion and laying it on a white paper towel. Press with your finger and see if any color bleeds onto the towel. If it does, return it to the store and try again. I've had good luck with DMC but occasionally I launder a redwork project and the thread bleeds.

8. Add two inches all around your design to accommodate your hoop and allow for seams in your finished project.

9. Kona cotton is available in white, off-white and black. It is densely woven and works well for embroidery. For embroidery and appliqué, avoid tightly woven broadcloth and polyester-cotton blends.

10. To avoid a filled-in, solid look in outline embroidery, use a "back" stitch when lines run close together. This is slightly narrower than the "stem" stitch.

11. Make stitches as even as possible. When you begin, don't worry that your stitches are long. Learn to control the needle to create even stitches and then worry about small stitches.

12. My favorite needle is the Colonial crewel #10 or embroidery #10. These are thin and easy to drive through the fabric and they have long eyes, making it easier to thread them.

13. Thread several needles at once to avoid stopping while you're working to re-thread.

14. Re-thread when the floss begins to thin. This ensures that the first and last stitch are the same width and look similar.

15. I recommend a wooden embroidery hoop. When placing it, be careful to avoid pulling threads or squashing your embroidery. Important: as you move the hoop, <u>first</u> undo the screw on the side. Next, carefully place the bottom of the hoop under the portion of the design to be worked. Gently lay the top of the loosened, enlarged hoop over embroidery. Finally, tighten the screw. Don't try to force the tightened top of the hoop over embroidery.

16. To finish embroidery pieces: hand launder, using gentle soap like Orvus (available at rural feed stores) or Quilt Soap (available at quilt shops). Drip-dry on a towel rack. Layer two terrycloth towels on the ironing board. While the embroidered piece is still damp, set the iron to medium heat, and gently press from the back of the embroidered piece. Spray starch if desired. If you're working on black, use a flake-free starch like Mary Ellen's.

Flower Dance | 19

Flower Dance

78" x 91" | Thirty 10" blocks

You Will Need:

- 2 1/2 yards green for sashing

- 6 1/2 yards black fabric for background
  I used only Kona Cotton black for the flowers' backgrounds; it is a deep, rich black that makes the flowers' colors pop.

- 1/8 yard each flower fabric
  As though you were creating an artist's palette, before you begin, purchase a wide range of colors. For the flowers, I used Moda "Marbles," by Patrick Lose. Other fabric lines have light and dark highlights. Some suggestions of Moda Marbles:

    - red (#6854)
    - dark red (#9865)
    - olive green (#322)
    - light green (#90)
    - light yellow (#29)
    - dark yellow (#33)
    - white (#65)
    - very light yellow (#36)
    - dark violet (#13)
    - light violet (#9856)
    - fuchsia (#9869)
    - pink (#9860)
    - light pink (#9802)
    - bright green (#9881-41)
    - orange (#9881-34)
    - gold (#33)
    - dark green (#9867)
    - bright orange (#9881-59)
    - gold (#9880-76)

Moda is always adding or changing their fabrics to coordinate with today's quilts and numbers may change. So consult the quilt and match your fabric choices to the colors I used. Do all thirty blocks or choose only a few — you will have a blooming treat.

- Embroidery thread: Choose appropriate colors for each flower.
- (Patterns and embroidery directions for each block are on pages 42 through 101. See embroidery stitches on 40, 41. Numbers on flowers refer to order of placement.)

Cutting the Blocks

- Start with 12" blocks. *(After appliquéing and embroidering the blocks, trim the blocks to measure 10 ½" square.)*
- Cut 2 outer border strips from black fabric: two 7 ½" x 80 ½" for the top and the bottom and two 7 ½" x 90" strips for the sides. Note: these measurements have been enlarged to allow for mitering the outer borders, if desired.
- Cut sashing strips.
  - Cut ninety-eight 1 ½" x 10 ½" green strips.
  - Cut forty nine 1 ½" x 10 ½" black strips.
  - Cut eighty 1 ½" green squares.
  - Cut one hundred 1 ½" black squares.
  - Cut two 1 ½" x 62 ½" green strips for top and bottom inner sashing.
  - Cut two 1 ½" x 77 ½" strips for inner sashing on both sides.

Assembly

- Arrange blocks on a large surface, balancing colors. Evenly space red flowers, pink, blue, etc., for harmonious placement. Group into five vertical rows. Mark numbers on the back or draw a diagram to avoid confusion when assembling quilt.
- To assemble the quilt top, sew three 10 ½" x 1 ½" strips together, lengthwise, making a strip set, with a black strip as the center and two green strips on each side. Repeat, using the rest of the 10 ½" strips.
- Make vertical rows, alternating 10" appliqué blocks and strip sets. Press seams toward the green strips. Repeat.
- To make "posts," sew five 1 ½" black squares together with four 1 ½" green squares to form a Nine-Patch block. Repeat, making twenty Nine-Patch blocks.
- Sew six strip sets together by alternating with five Nine-Patch posts, to separate the next vertical row of blocks. Continue until the entire quilt is assembled.
- Around the entire outer edge, sew a 1 ½" green strip as an inner border. Sew the top and bottom strips first, then add the side strips. Sew a black 7 ½" outer border to the outer edge of quilt, mitering corners.

Borders

Optional: Appliqués in outer border Because the border flower design runs across the corner seams, the appliquéd portion has to be done after you finish attaching the outer border of the quilt. After the quilt is assembled, carefully press the quilt top from the back. Trace the floral border design. This includes your choice of any flowers and leaves used in the blocks and uses the same fabrics and appliqué methods you used in the individual blocks.

Quilt as desired.

Flower Dance Setting for blocks   Green - color 1   Black - color 2

					2					
					1					
2	1		1	2	1	Block	1	2	1	Block
		Block								
			1	2	1	2	1	2	1	2
			2	1	2	1	2	1	2	1
			1	2	1	2	1	2	1	2
		Block	1	2	1	Block	1	2	1	Block
			1	2	1	2	1	2	1	2
			2	1	2	1	2	1	2	1
			1	2	1	2	1	2	1	2

Good Morning Pillowcases

Standard: 20" x 26"

These cases are the perfect gift for a bride, child or friend. If you make a quilt, make pillowcases from fabric that coordinates with your bedroom décor and embroider morning glories on the hem.

You Will Need:

- 7/8 yard fabric for base of pillowcase
- 1/3 yard fabric for hem of pillowcase
- 2" x 42" contrasting fabric for trim

Hem and Embroidery

- Cut hem band 9 ½" x 42 ½".
- Fold in half both directions. Find the center of the bottom left quarter for the embroidery motif. Measure the morning glory design (p. 62) to find the center and mark it with a pin. Place the morning glory line drawing underneath the center of the hem band's bottom left quarter, matching both centers.

- Trace the design.
- Stitch, using outline stitch and 2 or 3 strands of embroidery floss. Set hem aside.

Base of Pillowcase

- Cut base fabric 42" x 27".
- Right sides together, sew the 42" side of the embroidered band to the unembroidered 42" end of the pillowcase base. Press seam allowances toward the hem.

- Fold right sides together, stitch along the other end of the pillowcase base and up the side, sewing through both base and hem. Press the seam open.

- Fold the raw edge of the hem band down ¼" (wrong sides together). Press.
- Bring the folded edge to meet the hem band and base of pillowcase seam (wrong sides together). Pin. Stitch down to secure. Turn pillowcase.

Trim

- Cut the contrasting trim fabric strip 2" x 42".
- Press ¼" along both lengths of the strip. Then fold in half lengthwise and press. Pin the strip to cover the seam separating hem band and base of pillowcase. Top-stitch on both long sides of trim strip. Where both ends of strip meet, turn by hand and stitch down with 5 or 6 small stitches. Press.

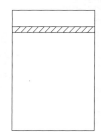

Mrs. Cleaver's Geranium Apron

Aprons are so popular and practical! Perfect for culinary masterpieces, entertaining, or making crafts, this cheery apron is a great gift.

Make sure there is enough space on the skirt to attach two pockets. I lined my apron's pockets and bib with bleached muslin and starched the finished garment to give it more body.

Young Chef's apron instructions are on page 37.

You Will Need:

- For apron, 2 yards cotton (Prewash fabric.)
- For yoke and pockets, 1/3 yard contrasting fabric
- For Geraniums, Moda "Marbles" red #9880-92 and green #9880-90
- Optional — 1 yard bleached muslin to line apron skirt, bib, and pockets (prewash fabric)
- Fusing — 1/8 yard Pellon Wonder-Under or Heat 'n Bond Lite
- Embroidery — DMC embroidery floss: #321 (Christmas red) and #3363 (grassy green)
- Spray starch, if desired, when apron is completed

Note: If you embroider around the geranium's fused petals and leaves, use a #8 or #9 crewel or embroidery needle. The #10 needles bend when stitching through fabric and fusible layers.

Cutting Instructions

- Geranium appliqué (pattern on page 64)

From apron fabric:

- Cut out one 11 ½" square piece for the apron bib.
- For the skirt, cut a rectangle 36 ½" x 34".
- For the waist sash, cut one 92" x 4" strip. (Piece three 4" x width of fabric pieces.)
- For arm sashes, cut two strips 3" x 75". (Piece four 3" x width of fabric pieces.)

From contrast fabric:

- Cut one 12 ½" x 3" piece for decorating the apron bib.
- Cut two 8 ½" x 9 ½" pockets.

From lining fabric:

- Cut one 11 ½" square to line apron bib.
- Cut two 9 ½" x 8 ½" pieces to line pockets.

Assembly

- Place lining and bib wrong sides together. Turn the contrasting fabric long edge under and top-stitch to the bib. Set aside.
- Trace the geranium design onto the pockets.
- Follow the fusible directions to fuse the geranium fabric (petals and leaves where the design indicates). Trace designs of petals and leaves onto fusible web. Cut out petals and leaves and fuse to the base (pocket) fabric. If desired, after fusing, using an outline or stem stitch and embroidery floss, and stitch around each petal and leaf, including the leaves' veins.
- To finish the pockets, lay the wrong sides of the pocket and pocket lining together. Stitch ¼" from the edge, leaving 2" for turning. Turn the pocket right side out and press.
- Position the appliquéd pockets 6" from the top of the apron skirt (the 36 ½" x 34" rectangle) and 4 ½" apart.
- Top-stitch the pocket onto the apron skirt.
- Gather along the top edge of the apron by sewing long stitches and pulling the thread to gather.
- Turn the skirt sides under ¼", press. Turn again, 1", press, and top-stitch.
- Turn up the hem 2 ½" and top-stitch.
- Turn the edges of the waist sash under ¼"; press. Fold the sash in half; fold the ends under ¼" and top-stitch along one long side, close to the edge of the sash.
- For the arm sashes, turn the edges under ¼". Press. Fold in half, lengthwise, and top-stitch close to the outer edges. Attach the arm sashes to the bib of the apron on the sides and top-stitch.
- Attach the bib to the top of the skirt by basting. Pin the waist sash to the skirt and bib. Top-stitch along the long edge that is not top-stitched, catching the bib and the skirt between the folded sash. Attach the arm sashes to the back of the waist sash 16" from the center of the apron bib.

Tulip Garden Shopper's Tote

14" x 16"

Everyone is going green these days and shopping with reusable, fabric totes! This speedy project will become a favorite. You may want to make one for everyone you know! The tote may be used over and over for shopping but it's also a great diaper bag, traveler's carry-on or a gardener's tote because it's washable. I combined the best characteristics of many bags for this project. You'll find that the wide straps in this pattern are much more comfortable than narrow ones, especially if you tote heavy groceries.

You Will Need:

- 2 yards green leaf print cotton for the body of the tote, inner pocket and lining
- 1/3 yard black cotton fabric
- 1/8 yard pink batik
- 1/8 yard green batik
- 1 yard interfacing (iron-on works well)
- Coordinating sewing thread in pink and green for buttonhole stitch on outer pocket appliqué

  Note: I chose Mettler Silk Finish Cotton thread in pink and green in shades that were lighter in color than my fabrics, to create silky highlights.

- Coordinating sewing thread to construct tote and for top-stitching
- Black sewing thread for top-stitching outer pocket
- Pellon's Wonder Under
- Floriani stabilizer

Cutting Instructions

- Cut four 14 ½" x 16 ½" rectangles from green print.
- Cut two 6" x 33" green print strips for the handles.
- Cut a 9 ½" square of black fabric for the pocket.
- Cut 9 ½" black square for pocket lining.
- Cut tulip appliqué pieces. (pattern on page 31)
- Optional: 6" square for inside pocket

Assembly

- Begin with the outer pocket. For the pocket appliqué I substituted pink batik instead of the original red marbled fabric for the petals, and green batik for the leaves and stems. I fused petals, stems, and leaves with Pellon's Wonder Under and machine embellished the edges, using an open-toe presser foot and machine buttonhole stitch. To stabilize the base fabric as I sewed the buttonhole stitch, I pinned tear-away Floriani stabilizer under my work, removing it when finished. For this project, I used batiks because there was no hand sewing required as in the other appliqués in this book. I used a medium weight iron-on interfacing on all portions of the tote to give it more body.

- Line the outer pocket to give it more stability by cutting a 9 ½" black square and stitching around the edges of the appliquéd block, leaving a 3" opening at the bottom. Turn, press and top-stitch in black thread.

- To construct the bag, cut four 14 ½" x 16 ½" rectangles from green print. Attach the outer pocket to the right side of the front of the tote by stitching over the previous top-stitching on three sides, leaving the top open.

- Sew two of the rectangles right sides together, along three sides, leaving the top open. Repeat with the other two rectangles. Turn one unit, wrong side out and one unit right side out.

- Press along the top of both units, ¼" from the open edge. Press toward the wrong side of units to form the hem.

- Nest one inside of the other, so that the wrong sides are together. Top-stitch both units together, ¼" from pressed top edges.

- For the handles, cut two 6" x 33" green print strips. Along long edges, turn under ¼", fold in half lengthwise. Wrong sides together, sew strips together along long edges, turn and press, topstitch. Turn the raw edges of the handle ends under ¼" and press.

- Attach the handles to the top of the bag and pin on each side. Stitch a square and then an "x" in the square to insure that the straps are securely fastened to the bag. Top-stitch around the handles and opening with one or two rows of stitching.

Friendship's Blossoms Table Runner

20" x 45"

Everyone needs a table runner to brighten a home! This quick-to-make project celebrates flowers and friendship. These bright colors work well for festive spring and summer tables but try using the "Poinsettia" block with holiday fabrics for an entirely different look. A white poinsettia on a dark green background would be smashing on a holiday table.

You Will Need:

- 1/3 yard light fabric for background squares (I used white Kona cotton.)
- 1¼ yard print for border, binding and star points
- ½ yard setting fabric
- 1/4 yard green "frame" fabric to sash around the embroidered blocks and for the center of the "Friendship Star" block
- 3/4 yard backing fabric
- Coordinating sewing thread
- Green DMC embroidery floss DMC #367
- Yellow DMC embroidery floss DMC #744
- Gold DMC embroidery floss DMC #3821
- Brown or black DMC embroidery floss DMC #4
- Bright gold DMC embroidery floss DMC #3820
- 22" x 44" Cotton batting

Cutting Instructions

- For the Friendship Star (center) block, cut two 3 7/8" squares from the light (background) fabric and two 3 7/8" squares from the print fabric. Then cut four 3 ½" squares from the light fabric and one 3 ½" square from the green.
- For the embroidered blocks, cut two 11" white background fabric squares.
- For <u>each</u> of the two blocks, cut two 2" x 7" and two 2" x 10" green "framing" strips.
- Cut two 9 7/8" squares from the setting fabric. Cut each square once diagonally, to create four side triangles.
- Cut one 10 ¼" square. Cut diagonally twice to create four corner triangles.

Note: you may piece these strips, or you may need to cut an additional 4 ½" strips, depending on the width of your fabric.

Assembly

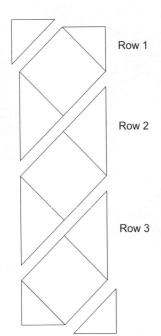

Row 1

Row 2

Row 3

- On the two 11" white background fabric squares, trace the desired embroidery designs and embroider, using one color or several colors, using the "outline" or "stem" stitch. Press, starch (optional), and trim blocks to 7".

- Attach the 2" green "framing" strips (two 7" and two 10") to all four sides of each block. True up the blocks to 9 ½" square.

- Draw a diagonal line on the backs of the two 3 7/8" light squares. Place one light square on top of a 3 7/8" print square, right sides together. Sew ¼" on each side of the line. Cut apart on the line and press. Repeat with the two remaining 3 7/8" squares. Arrange the blocks in the Star pattern, adding the four light 3 ½" squares and the one green center square. Sew together in rows. Then sew the rows together. Trim to 9 ½".

- Row 1: Sew one side setting triangle to the bottom left of the top embroidered block. Sew one corner triangle to the top right of the block. Press.

- Row 2: Sew one side triangle to the top right and one to the bottom left of the pieced Friendship Star block. Press.

- Row 3: Sew one side triangle to the top right of the second embroidered block. Sew a corner triangle to the lower left side of the block. Press.

- Sew the three rows together. Add the two remaining corner triangles. Press. Trim sides.

Borders

- Cut two border strips 4 ½" x the width of the center and sew one on the top and one on the bottom of the table runner.

- Cut two border strips 4 ½" x the length of the center and sew on each side. Press. Trim.

Back, Quilt and Bind

- After piecing the runner top, pin-baste the backing, cotton batting and the top.

- Quilt by hand or machine, trim the edges, and bind. *Note: I machine-quilted ¼" around each of the pieced portions of the runner in white thread and, in the green frames, I quilted ¼" from the seam line in green thread.*

- For binding, cut a strip 2 ½" x 45" and press in half, lengthwise. Place binding strip on the top side of the runner. Line up the raw edge of the binding with the edge of the table runner. Sew ¼" from the raw edges through all thicknesses. Turn the binding and whipstitch, using matching thread.

Young Chef's Flower Power Apron

Your beginner cook needs a cover-up for spills and splatters. My niece Cecilia loved her first apron and wore it when she washed dishes as a pre-schooler. Now, age 12, she's an accomplished cook with her own recipes.

To miniaturize the geranium design to child-size, I chose only a few petals, stems, and two leaves and appliquéd those onto the pocket using Wonder Under fusible.

You Will Need:

- ¾ yard 100% cotton fabric for apron and ties
- 1/4 yard contrasting 100% cotton fabric for pocket and yoke (Prewash fabrics. The apron will be washed often.)
- DMC embroidery floss in #321 (red) and #3363 (green)
- For geraniums: 1/8 yard each of Moda "Marbles" in #9880-92 red and #9880-90 green
- 1/8 yard Pellon
- Wonder Under fusible

Cutting Instructions

From apron fabric

- Cut three strips: one 3" x 18" for the neck strap and two strips 3" x 17" for the apron ties.
- Cut fabric 20" x 23" for the body of the apron.

From contrast fabric

- Cut a strip 4" x 11" as a yoke.
- Cut a 4 ½" x 5" piece for the pocket.

Assembly

- Apron ties — Press ½" along the two long sides and on the end of the strips. Fold in half lengthwise. Top-stitch close to both edges. Set aside.
- Fuse the geranium design onto the 4 ½" x 5" piece, and embellish as desired. Turn the sides and bottom under ½" and press.
- To shape the apron, measure 16" from the hem and cut both sides on a thirty degree angle toward the center of the apron's top. Turn the edges under ½" and topstitch to secure the top of the apron.
- Fold the 4" x 11" yoke in half; press. Top stitch to the apron to secure the yoke.
- Attach the neck and side ties as shown. Hem the bottom by turning ½" and then 2". Machine stitch.
- Pin the pocket in place in the center of the apron. Top stitch close to the edges of the pocket.

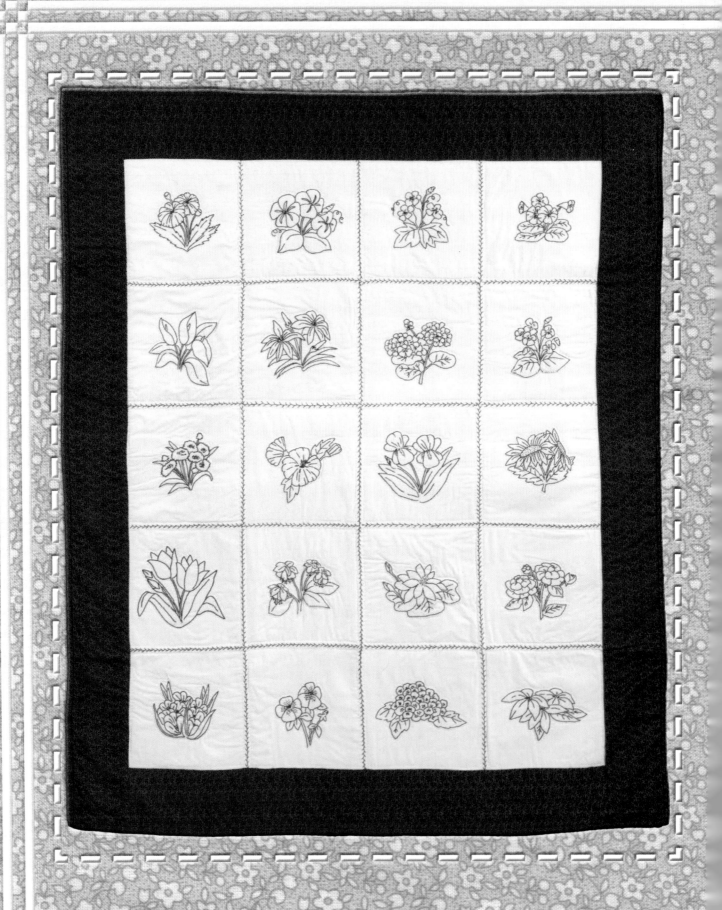

Redwork Throw or Wall Quilt

46" x 55"

Popular since the 1860's when the Victorians studied flowers and red dye became colorfast, redwork embroidery makes a striking, visually appealing, quilt. I chose twenty of my favorite flowers for this small quilt. You can add more blocks or use just a few for a table runner or wall quilt.

You Will Need:

- 2 ⅓ yards white solid cotton for each block (Kona cotton in white is my choice) Cut 12 squares.
- 2 yards border fabric
- 3 skeins DMC #498 red embroidery floss
- #10 embroidery or crewel needles
- Embroidery hoop
- Embroidery scissors or snips
- Red Gelly Roll pen
- ½ yard fabric for binding
- 3 yards for backing (must be pieced)
- Batting

Assembly

- Using a light box or a window on a sunny day, trace the flower design onto the background fabric. Use masking tape to securely hold the design in place.
- Using two strands of embroidery floss, embroider the design.
- Trim the finished block to 9 ½".
- Arrange the blocks in a pleasing manner — heavily embroidered designs should alternate with simpler ones.
- Sew the blocks together in rows.
- Along the seam lines, embroider the "feather" or "briar" stitch to divide blocks.
- Press on the wrong side of the finished quilt with a bath towel underneath and starch, if desired. *An alternative finish—add 1 ½" sashing strips between blocks to enlarge the quilt and to separate blocks. In that case, increase the yardage for backing.*
- Cut borders at 5 ½" x 36" for the top and bottom and 5 ½" X 55" for the sides. Sew them to the center in that order.
- Layer the quilt top, batting, and backing. Quilt ¼" from briar stitching and quilt around flowers. Bind.

Redwork Embroidery Stitches

Stem or Outline stitch

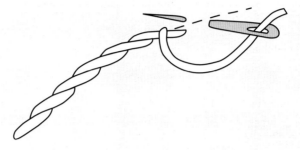

Straight or Running stitch

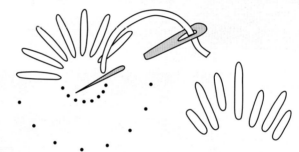

Blanket or Buttonhole stitch

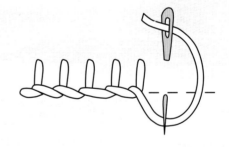

Briar or Feather stitch

A

B

Lazy Daisy

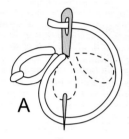

A

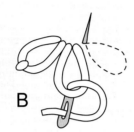

B

French knot

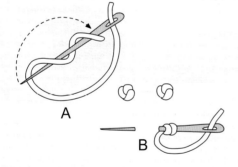

A

B

Back stitch

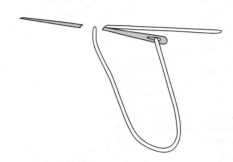

Satin stitch

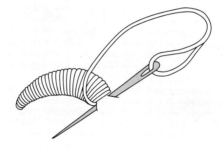

Whip stitch

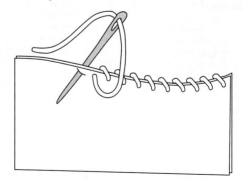

Hollyhock

(Row 1, Block 1) Trace hollyhock designs onto background fabric and proceed as in general directions. Embroider the outline stitch in dark red floss for petals' veins, olive green floss in outline stitch for leaves' veins, and 1/8" yellow straight stitches for centers. Accent centers with black French knots.

Color guide: Leaves: Moda Marbles #9877 Petals: #9865

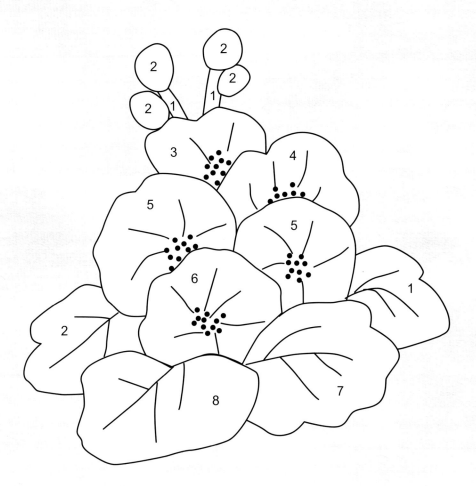

Coneflower

(Row 1, Block 2) Trace coneflower designs onto background fabric and proceed as in general directions. Embroider outline stitch in medium green thread for leaves' veins and fuchsia floss for petals. Stitch approximately forty French knots in brown floss as the flowers' centers.

Color guide: Leaves: olive green – Moda Marbles #322 Petals: fuchsia #9869

Calla Lily

(Row 1, Block 3) Trace calla lily designs onto background fabric and proceed as in general directions. Embroider outline stitch in bright green floss for the leaves' veins. Instead of appliquéing the stamen in the center of the flower, embroider it, using a "satin" stitch in bright yellow floss.

Color guide: Leaves: dark green – Moda Marbles #9867 Petals: white #9880-52

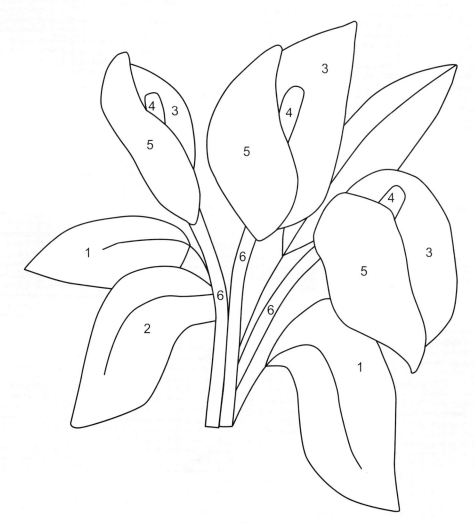

Petunia

(Row 1, Block 4) Trace petunia designs onto background fabric and proceed as in general directions. Embroider divisions between petunia petals with outline stitch in fuchsia floss and leaves' veins in outline stitch in green floss.

Color guide: Leaves: Green Moda Marbles #9881 41 Petals: #9869

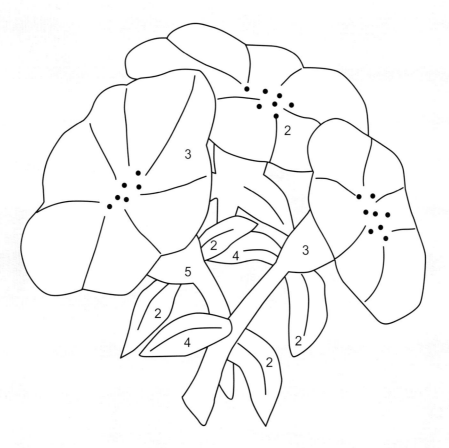

Bachelor Button

(Row 1, Block 5) Trace bachelor button blossoms onto background fabric. After appliquéing the blossom, to create the "fringed" appearance of the flower, use embroidery. Use blue floss to match petals and make approximately thirty-five small, straight stitches radiating around the blossom. The stitches should appear random, set at various angles, radiating from the flower onto the black background fabric. Embroider center with ¼" straight stitches, radiating from flowers' centers, using one strand of black floss and then one strand of white floss.

Color guide: Leaves: bright green - Moda Marbles # 9880-90 Petals: medium blue – #9809

Trumpet Vine

(Row 2, Block 1) Trace trumpet vine's designs onto background fabric and proceed as in general directions. The trumpet vine's centers are embroidered with 7-8 small black French knots, and the tendrils and veins of the leaves are embroidered in bright green floss, using the outline stitch.

Color guide: Leaves: Moda Marbles #9867 Petals: #9881

Iris

(Row 2, Block 2) Trace iris designs onto background fabric and proceed as in general directions. For iris "beards," embroider ¼" straight stitches at 45 degree angles, using light yellow floss and black floss. Stitch leaves' veins in outline stitch, using bright green floss.

Color guide: Leaves: Moda Marbles #9881-41 Petals: #9856 & #9850

Clematis

(Row 2, Block 3) Trace clematis designs onto background fabric and proceed as in general directions. Embroider outline stitch in dark green embroidery floss for leaves' veins and dark purple for petals' veins.

Color guide: Petals: dark purple — Moda Marbles #9880-13 Leaves: dark green – #9867

Tulip

(Row 2, Block 4) Trace tulips' designs onto background fabric and proceed as in general directions. The tulips' leaves are made with two colors of green. The top of the leaves is made with a light green and the bottom in a bright green. Embroider leaves' veins in light green floss.

Color guide: Leaves: Moda Marbles #9881 41 and #90   Petals: #9880-92

Day Lily

(Row 2, Block 5) Trace day lily designs onto background fabric and proceed as in general directions. Embroider outline stitch in bright gold floss for veins in petals and lines in buds. For pistils, use one strand of brown and one strand of yellow floss together in the "outline" stitch. At the top of each pistil, stitch a French knot.

Color guide: Leaves: Moda Marbles #9880-23 Petals and buds: #9870

Morning Glory

(Row 3, Block 1) Trace morning glory designs onto background fabric and proceed as in general directions. Embroider tendrils and veins of leaves in light green floss. Embroider divisions of petals in light blue floss. Embroider lines on the buds in a darker blue. Embroider 7-9 small French knots in black floss for centers of flowers.

Color guide: Leaves: Moda Marbles 9881-67 Petals: #9881-27

Geranium

(Row 3, Block 2) Trace geranium designs onto background fabric and proceed as in general directions. Embroider outline stitch in red for petals, French knots in yellow for blossoms' centers, and outline stitch in olive green for leaves.

Color guide: Petals: Moda Marbles #9881-68 Leaves: #9877

Pond Lily

(Row 3, Block 3) Trace pond lily designs onto background fabric and proceed as in general directions. Embroider the center of lily with the outline stitch in light yellow floss using short, straight stitches, and the leaves' veins using the outline stitch in light green embroidery floss.

Color guide: Leaves: Moda Marbles #90 Petals: #9802

Cosmo

(Row 3, Block 4) Trace cosmos designs onto background fabric and proceed as in general directions. Embroider outline stitch in bright pink for veins in petals and medium green in veins of leaves. In flowers' centers, stitch ten or twelve French knots in yellow floss.

Color guide: Leaves: medium green – # 9877 Petals: bright pink #9804

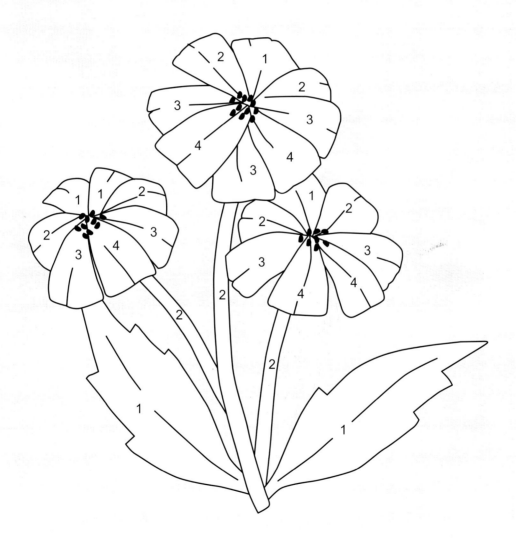

Poinsettia

(Row 3, Block 5) Trace poinsettia designs onto background fabric and proceed as in general directions. Embroider the centers of poinsettias with lime green French knots and small yellow French knots. Embroider petals' veins using the outline stitch in bright red floss and leaves' veins in medium green floss.

Color guide: Leaves: Moda Marbles #9867   Petals: #6854

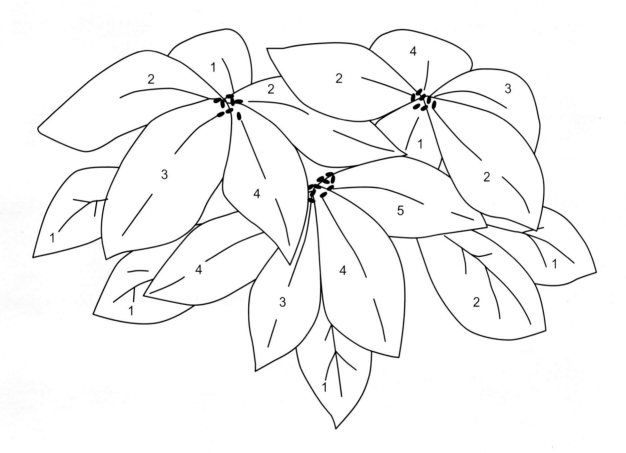

Zinnia

(Row 4, Block 1) Trace zinnia's designs onto background fabric and proceed as in general directions. The zinnias' ragged edges are made by using the straight stitch in bright pink floss. After appliquéing three oval shapes in bright pink, take three straight stitches per petal in a "u" shape—two on each side, one on the bottom.

Zinnias' centers are made with small French knots in yellow floss and three small straight stitches in black floss.

Color guide: Leaves: Moda Marbles #9881 Petals: #9869

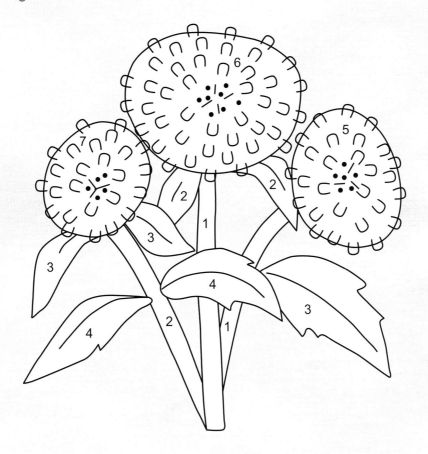

Jonquil

(Row 4, Block 2) Trace jonquil designs onto background fabric and proceed as in general directions. Embroider outline stitch in light yellow for petals' veins, olive green outline stitch for leaves' veins, and black and yellow French knots for pistils and stamens inside jonquil's "trumpet."

Color Guide: Leaves: Moda Marbles #9880-23 Petals: Moda #9870 (the trumpets' golden color) and #9881-29 (light yellow for outer petals)

Fuchsia

(Row 4, Block 3) Trace fuchsia designs onto background fabric and proceed as in general directions. Embroider outline stitch in olive green floss for leaves, bright pink for accents on fuchsia blossoms and black straight stitches for fuchsia pistils. At the end of each pistil, stitch a French knot in black.

Color guide: Petals: Moda Marbles (top fuchsia petals) #9869 and light pink #9802 (bottom petals) Leaves: medium green #9880-23

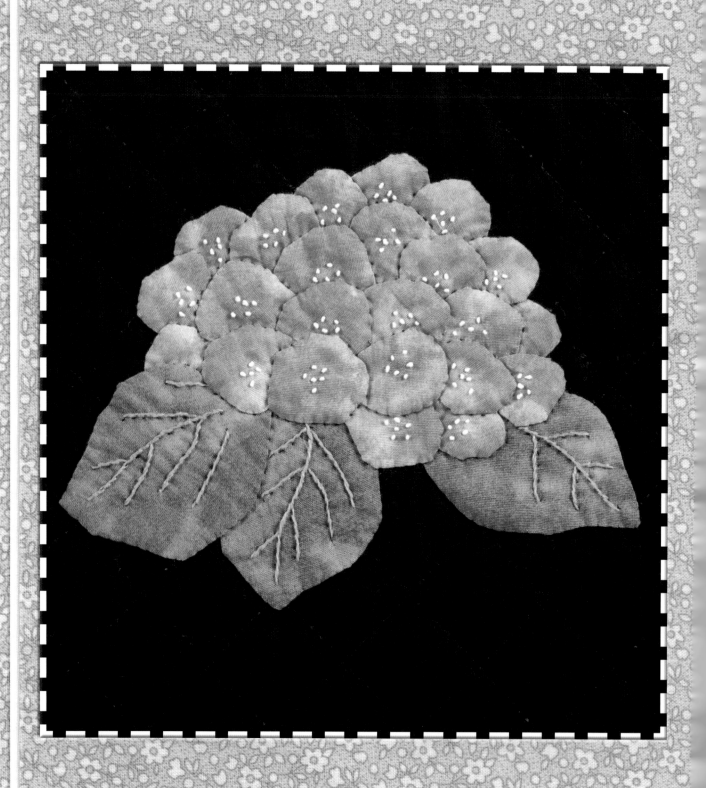

Hydrangea

(Row 4, Block 4) Trace hydrangea designs onto background fabric and proceed as in general directions. Use six or seven small French knots in white floss for centers of blossoms.

Color guide: Leaves: Moda Marbles #322 Petals: #9809

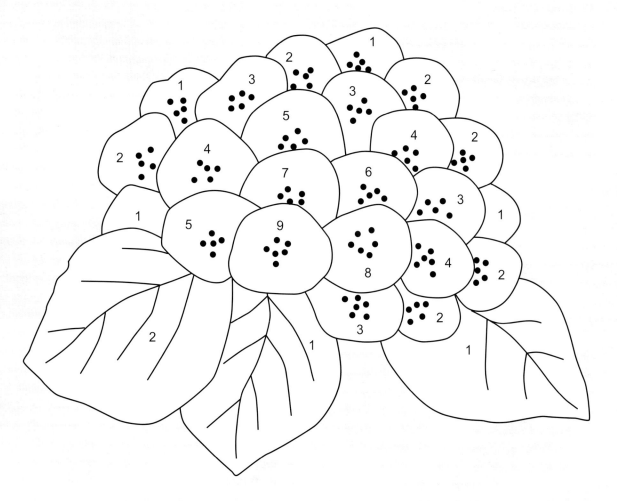

Sunflower

(Row 4, Block 5) Trace sunflower designs onto background fabric and proceed as in general directions. The sunflowers' centers are made of brown and the petals are made with gold fabric. Embroider French knots using two shades—medium brown and light yellow floss—for the sunflower seeds. Embroider petals' veins using the outline stitch with gold floss and veins in leaves in medium green floss.

Color guide: Leaves: Moda Marbles #9867 Petals: # 9880 76

Pansy

(Row 5, Block 1) Trace pansy designs onto background fabric and proceed as in general directions. Note: the top two petals in the flowers and the bud are made of light pink fabric. The bottom petals are in deep purple. Embroider the pansy "faces" with straight stitching of black floss. Centers of pansies are made of 4-5 yellow French knots. Embroider leaves' veins with medium green floss.

Color guide: Leaves: Moda Marbles # 9881 34 Bud and Top petals: #9856
Bottom petals: #9850

Rose

(Row 5, Block 2) Trace rose designs onto background fabric and proceed as in general directions. The rose is made of two different fabrics—dark pink or red for the flowers' and bud's centers and a medium pink for the outer petals.

Color guide: Leaves: Moda Marbles #322 Rose centers: #6854
Rose petals: #9860

Marigold

(Row 5, Block 3) Trace marigold designs onto background fabric and proceed as in general directions. Embroider outline stitch in gold floss in petals' leaves and green floss in leaves' veins. Stitch 6-10 small black French knots in centers of marigolds.

Color guide: Leaves: Moda Marbles #9880-84 Petals: #9880-47

Violet

(Row 5, Block 4) Trace violets' designs onto background fabric and proceed as in general directions. The violets' petals are made with two colors of purple. The top two petals are light purple; the bottom petals are dark purple. Embroider 3-4 small French knots in yellow in the centers and finish with 2-3 French knots in black floss. Embroider leaves' veins in the outline stitch.

Color guide: Leaves: Moda Marbles #322   Petals: Top petals #9880-95
Bottom petals: #9869

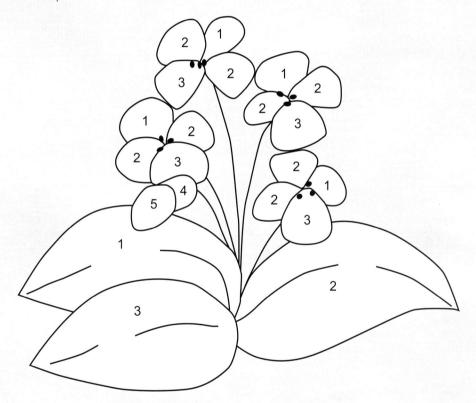

Poppy

(Row 5, Block 5) Trace poppy designs onto background fabric and proceed as in general directions. The center area is orange-red; the outer petals are bright red. Embroider center of poppy with 11-12 French knots in black floss. Embroider veins in petals using the outline stitch in bright orange floss and leaves' veins in medium green.

Color guide: Leaves: Moda Marbles #9881-28   Poppy Center: #9880-92 Poppy Outer petals: #9880-60

Crocus

(Row 6, Block 1) Trace crocus designs onto background fabric and proceed as in general directions. Embroider outline stitch in medium green for leaves' veins and very light yellow or white for veins in petals. In the crocus' centers, stitch 3 or 4 French knots in yellow.

Color guide: Leaves: – Moda Marbles #9877 Petals: light yellow — #9881-51

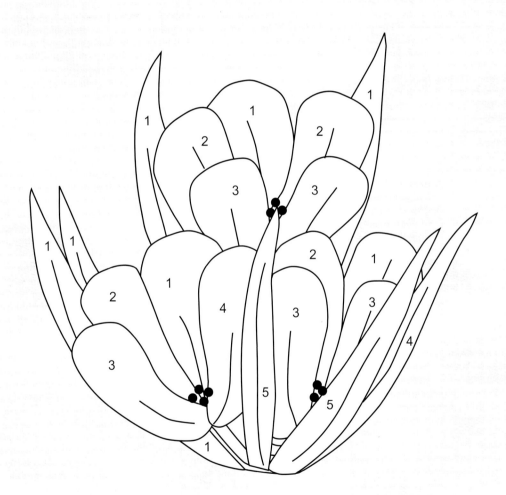

Nasturtium

(Row 6, Block 2) Trace nasturtium designs onto background fabric and proceed as in general directions. Embroider 4-5 small French knots in black floss and embroider outline stitch in green floss for leaves' veins.

Color guide: Leaves: Moda Marbles #9867 Petals: #9881 59

Daisy

(Row 6, Block 3) Trace daisy designs onto background fabric and proceed as in general directions. Embroider French knots in yellow floss for centers and olive green floss for leaves' veins.

Color guide: olive green - Moda Marbles #322 Petals: #9880-87

Hibiscus

(Row 6, Block 4) Trace hibiscus designs onto background fabric and proceed as in general directions. Use red floss in outline stitch for petals' veins, dark green floss in outline stitch for leaves' veins, and French knots in black for flowers' centers.

Color guide: Petals: Moda Marbles #6854   Leaves: # 9867

Tiger Lily

(Row 6, Block 5) Trace tiger lily's design onto background fabric and proceed as in general directions. The tiger lily's stamens are embroidered with black floss using the outline stitch and the leaves are embroidered in the outline stitch in a medium green. Each petal is embroidered with approximately 40 French knots in black floss and the petals' veins are embroidered in orange floss using the outline stitch.

Color guide: Leaves: Moda Marbles #322   Petals: #9881 34

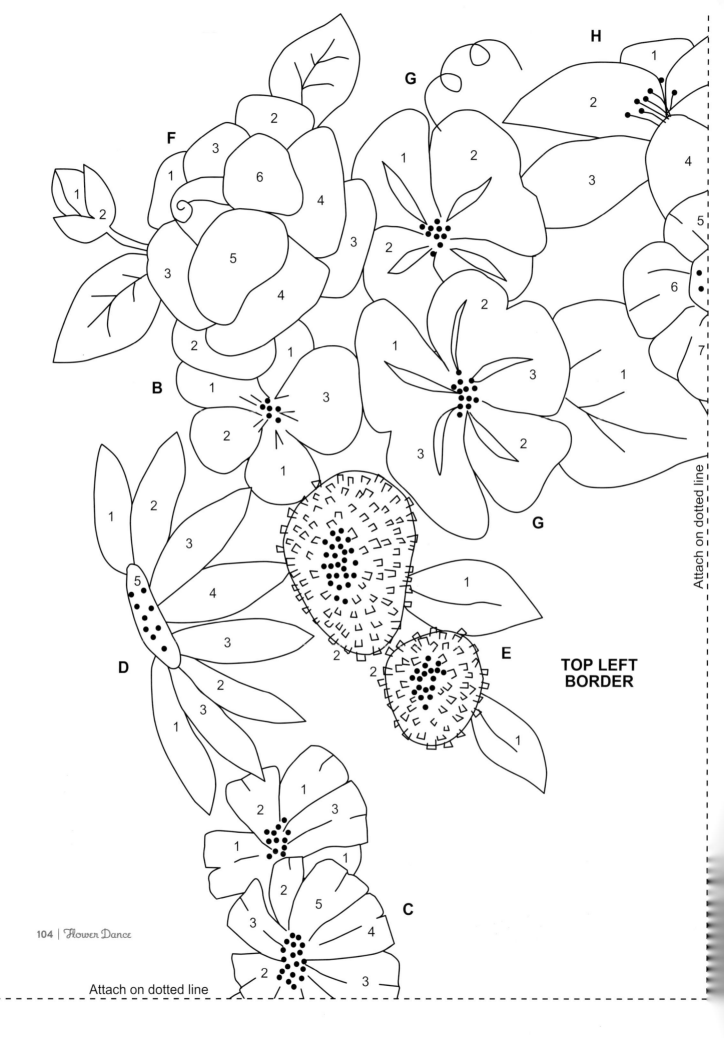

F

G

H

B

D

E

**TOP LEFT
BORDER**

C

Attach on dotted line

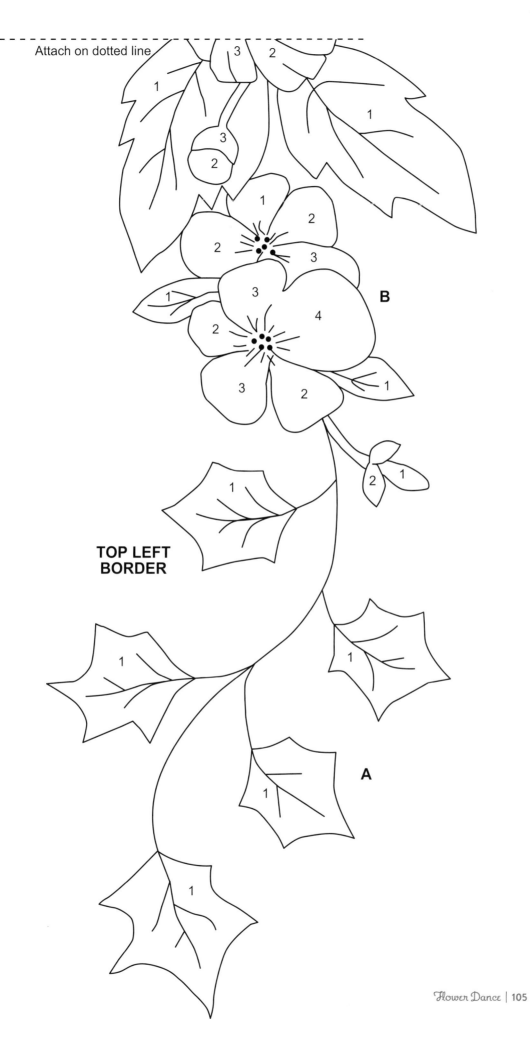

Attach on dotted line

B

TOP LEFT
BORDER

A

Attach on dotted line

Attach on dotted line

BOTTOM RIGHT
BORDER

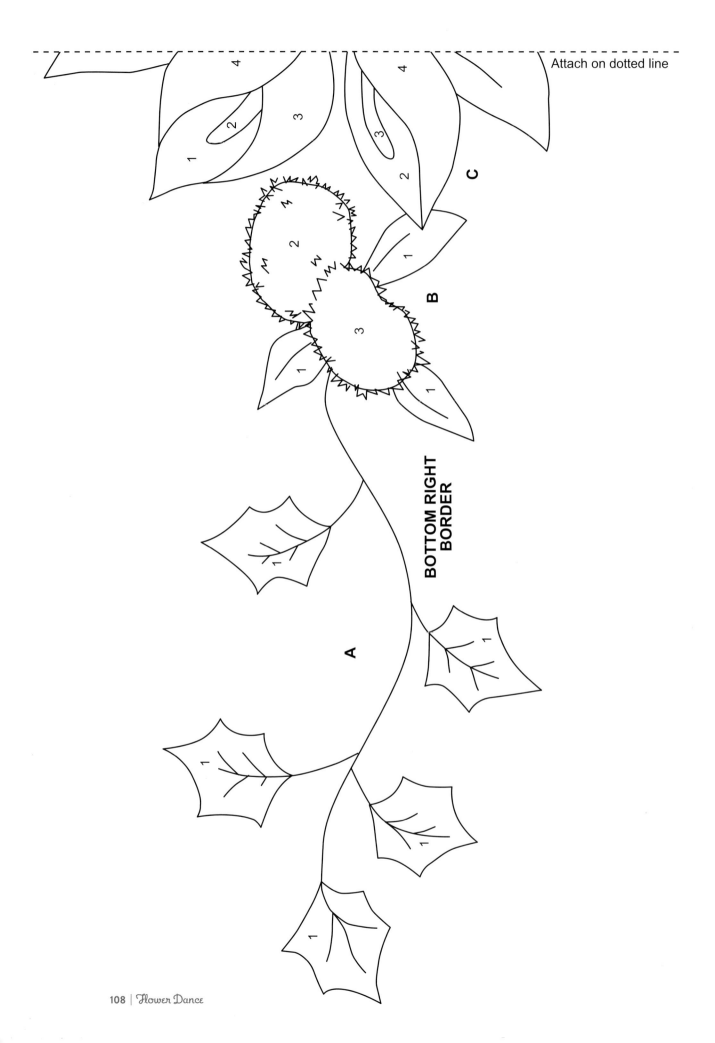

Attach on dotted line

BOTTOM RIGHT
BORDER

Attach on dotted line

BOTTOM RIGHT
BORDER

Border Appliqué

The appliqué flowers include eight flower varieties at the top left corner and at the bottom right border.

Top left Border

A - Ivy: Green fabric. Embroider the leaf veins and stems using an outline stitch.

B - Pansy: Top petals are light lavender fabric, bottom petals are dark purple. Embroider straight stitches in black floss, and French knots in centers in floss.

C - Daisy: White fabric for the petals and the bud, green for the stem, leaves and the bud's stem. Embroider yellow French knots in the centers. Embroider the petal veins in white.

D - Sunflower: Dark brown fabric for the center, gold for the petals. Mix one strand of yellow and one brown for French knots for the center. Embroider petal veins in gold floss.

E - Zinnia: Appliqué bright pink fabric in a circular shape to indicate the flower and then straight-stitch in U-shapes to create the ragged, small petals of the zinnia.

F - Rose: Center petal fabric is dark pink; outer petals and bud are lighter pink. Leaves are green. Embroider the centers of the flower in pink floss, the leaves veins in green.

G - Morning Glory: Blue fabric for petals and bud. Embroider lines on petals in blue floss; embroider tendril in green floss.

H - Day Lily: Yellow fabric for petals. Embroider veins with yellow floss. Centers are brown and yellow floss using straight stitches and French knots.

I - Poppy: Red fabric for outer leaves, green for the bud, orange for the centers. Embroider the petal veins with red floss. Leaves are green. Use French knots for poppy seeds.

Bottom Right Border

B - Bachelor Buttons: Blue fabric for a spherelike shape for the petal; embroider with blue floss and small straight stitches to create the shaggy edges of the flower. Green fabric for the leaves, embroider the veins in green floss. Centers: black French knots and white straight stitches.

C - Calla Lillies: White fabric for the petals, yellow for the throat, green for the leaves. Embroider veins in green.

D - Daffodils: Use darker yellow fabric for the trumpet (center) of the flower. Embroider French knots for the centers in black floss.

E - Coneflower: Fuchsia fabric for the petals. Brown French knots for the cone.

F - Clematis: Purple fabric for the petals and black French knots for the center. Embroider the petal veins in purple floss.

G - Tulip: Use two shades of red fabric for the petals, with the lighter shade on the top petal. Use the lighter shade for the bud. Use green fabric for the leaf and embroider the vein in green.

H - Cosmos: Use bright pink fabric for the petals and embroider French knots in black for the flower centers. Using matching floss, embroider the petal veins.

I - Iris: Use light purple fabric for the top three petals, dark purple for the bottom petals. Embroider, using a straight stitch, using yellow and black embroidery thread for the Iris "beards."

Resources

Needles:

- Colonial Needle Co. (distributors of John James, Hemmings and Colonial Needles, made in England to exacting standards) found in needlework and quilting stores. I recommend Kathy Delaney's Needle Sampler.

Scissors:

- Sharp, tapering appliqué scissors, Famore Cutlery at famorecutlery.com
- Dovo medium-sized sewing shears, imported from Germany. Dovo scissors are available at sewing and quilting stores that carry unusually precise and long-wearing products.

Thread:

- Gutermann silk
- YLI silk
- Aurifil 50 wt.
- Mettler Silk-Finish Cotton

Appliqué Fabrics:

- KonaCotton for base of appliqués, Moda "Marbles" in a variety of colors, or "Fusions" by Robert Kaufman

Roxanne's Glue Baste It:

- (now available through the Colonial Needle Co. and through craft and quilting stores) works to position appliqué pieces but must be rinsed out completely.

Books:

- Beth Ferrier's *Hand Appliqué by Machine*
- Alex Anderson's *Hand and Machine Appliqué*

Tear-Away Stabilizer:

- Floriani's Embroidery stabilizer (available at sewing and quilt shops)

Interfacing:

- "Pellon Wonder Under or Heat'N Bond Lite iron-on interfacing. It feels like muslin but has a fusible on one side.